DISCOVERIN
MT RAINIER
A Nature Activity Book

By
Nancy Field
Sally Machlis

Illustrated by Sally Machlis

Cover art by Michael Maydak

Published by Discover Your Northwest • Seattle, WA • discovernw.org
Discover Your Northwest promotes the discovery of Northwest public lands, enriches the experience of visitors, and builds community stewardship of these special places today and for generations to come.

ISBN 978-0-914019-80-0

Copyright © 2017 Discover Your Northwest
original copyright © 1980, 1992, 2008 Nancy Field and Sally Machlis
previously published by Dog-Eared Publications LLC.

Mount Rainier is so big that it can be seen from many places in Washington. It is higher than any other mountain in the state.

The entrances to Mount Rainier National Park are in the forest. As you follow the park road up the mountain, you will see many exciting changes. The weather is different near the top of the mountain, with colder temperatures and more snow. The trees, plants, and animals that can live high on the mountain are different than the ones you may find at the park entrances.

The forest is the home of many plants and animals. They are not always easy to see. Can you find the following plants and animals in this picture?

Bear	Douglas squirrel	Garter snake	Sword fern
Red fox	Porcupine	Stellar's jay	Douglas-fir tree
Raccoon	Black-tailed deer	Mushroom	Vine maple tree

The Longmire family were the first white settlers to live at Mount Rainier. They built a cabin in 1888, which is still standing. As guests began to arrive to use the hot mineral springs, a log hotel was built.

At Longmire it's fun for families to take the self-guided trail. They can see mineral springs, a beaver dam, and many plants and animals.

Can you find an alder tree that has been chewed on by the beaver?

Camping

Families often stay in the campgrounds—like Cougar Rock, Ohanapecosh, or Sunshine Point. It's fun to sit around the campfire cooking and singing.

Things to do in Camp

Pick Up Litter in Your Campground

How to Make a Box Oven

Line a cardboard box with heavy aluminum foil. Line another piece of cardboard and place inside on the bottom of the box. Place 4 empty soup cans or rocks inside the box so that a baking pan can be balanced on them. Carefully place about 6 hot briquettes of charcoal between the soup cans (or rocks). Set the baking pan on the soup cans over the hot briquettes. Close the lid to the box. It will take about 20 minutes to bake biscuits or a sheet cake. A meatloaf will take about 45 minutes. You may need to add more charcoal.

Recipe
Campfire Stew

Fry 1 lb. hamburger and 1 chopped onion until brown. Pour off fat. Add 1 can condensed vegetable soup and enough water to prevent sticking. Cover and cook until meat is cooked.

Recipe
GORP

(For energy while you hike)

Mix together:

1 bag M & M's
1 jar peanuts
1 box raisins

Recipe
Bread on a Stick

Blend biscuit mix and water to make a stiff dough, or use canned biscuits. Mold it over a greased stick. Cook and brown slowly over coals. Pull biscuit off the stick and eat with butter, jam, or honey.

Listen to a Naturalist Talk at an Evening Program

Backpacking

Not everyone camps in a campground. Backpackers carry everything they need when they hike to explore the wilderness. They sleep in the tent they carry with them, or in the shelters that have been built along the trails. Sometimes they sleep without a shelter, under the stars.

Wonderland Trail Game

The Wonderland Trail is a path for hikers which goes all the way around Mount Rainier. It is over 90 miles long, traveling through forests, up to alpine meadows, and even higher to the bare rocks and snow of the rugged mountain.

How to play:

1. The object of the game is to be the first player to return to Sunrise.

2. Each player needs to find their own playing piece on the ground. Find a small pebble, or maybe a twig, or a cone, which looks different from other players' markers. Place it at start.

3. Find 4 more pebbles and number them 1, 2, 3, and 4 using a pencil, crayon, or whatever you can find to make a mark. Place them in a container, like a paper bag or a hat. When it is your turn, draw a pebble from the container and move the number of squares written on the pebble.

4. Follow the special instructions on the board.

   Turn the page to find the game.

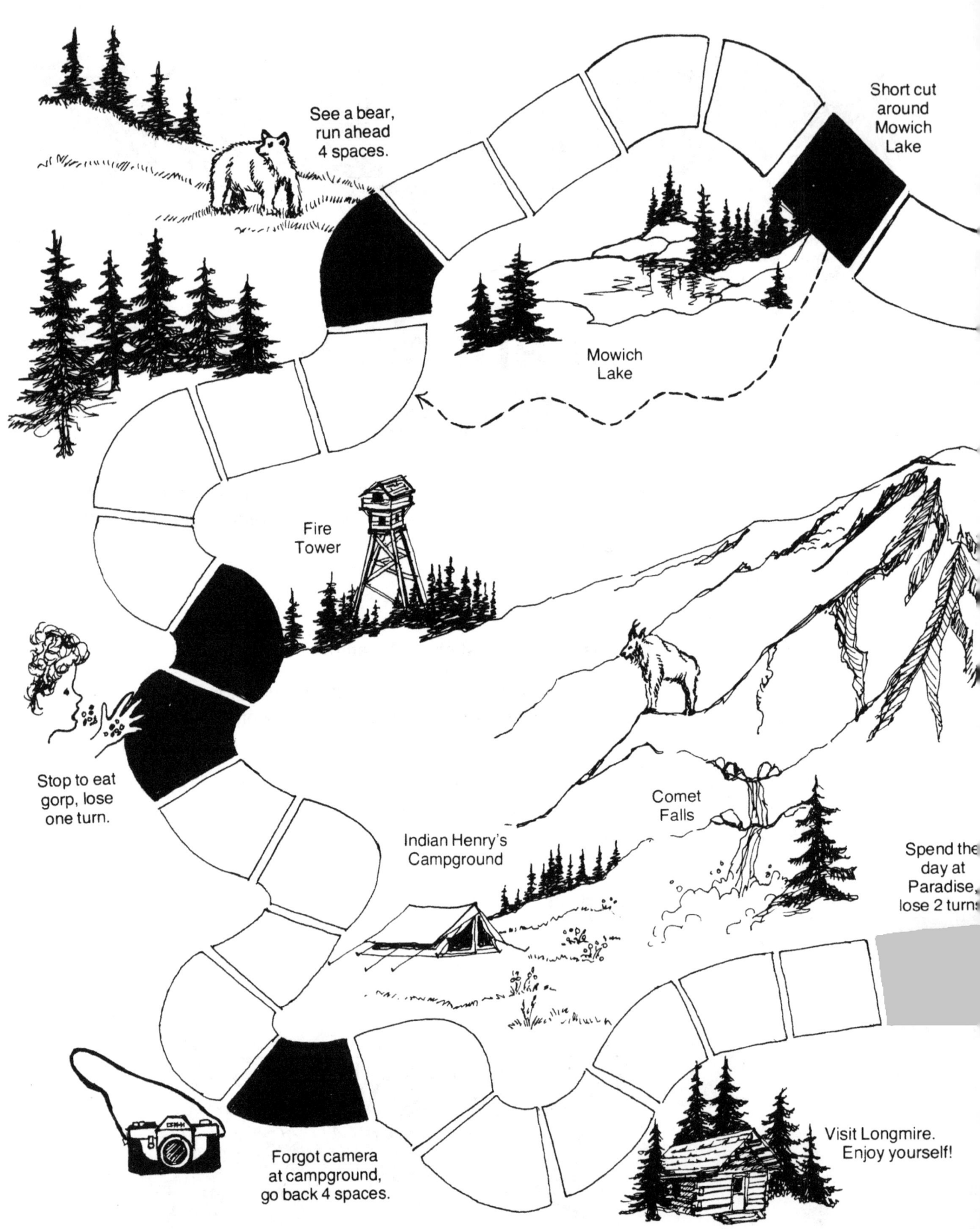

Waterfall Game

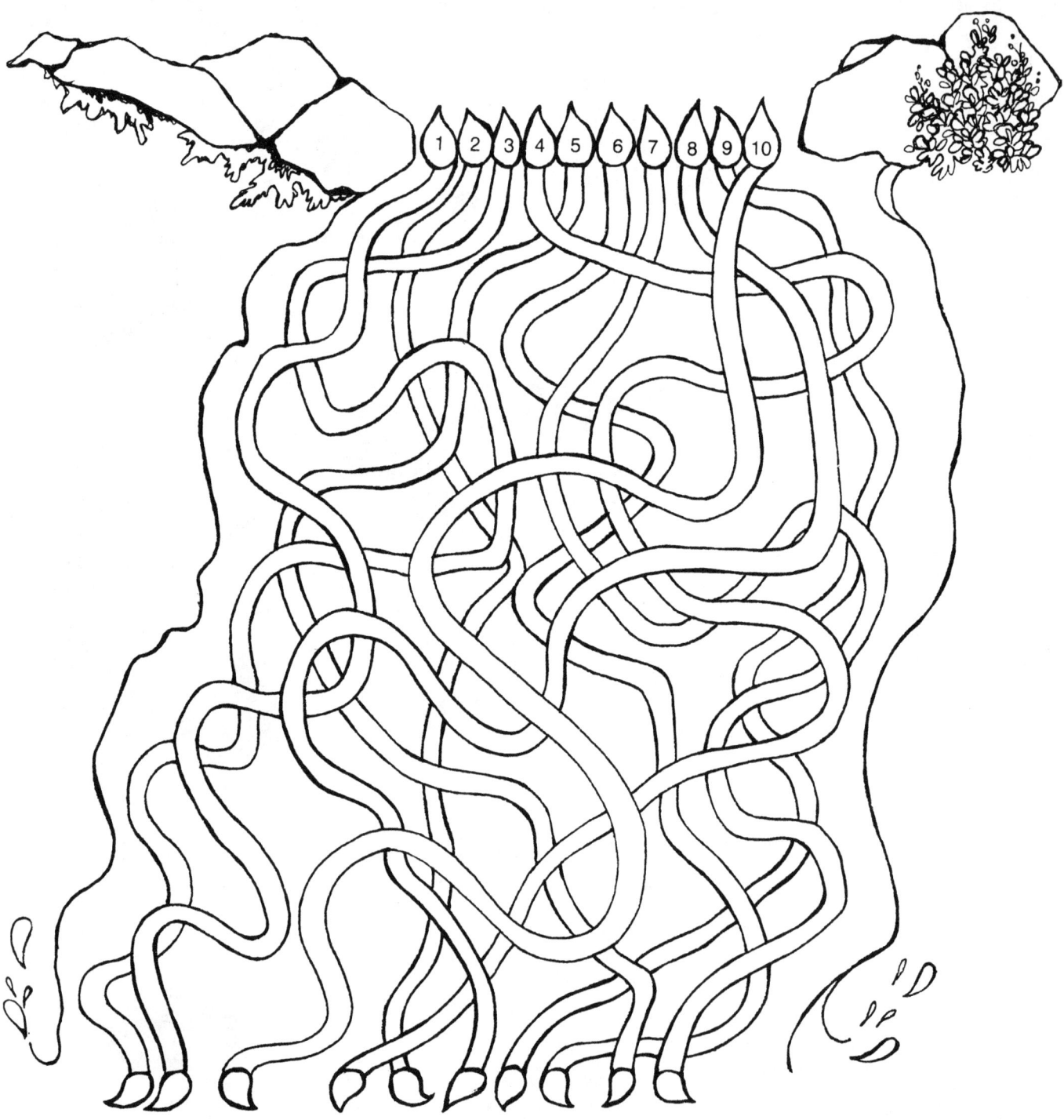

The park has many beautiful waterfalls. The water finds its way from springs and melting snow, down the waterfall, to the rivers below.

Can you follow the drops of water through the maze from the top to the bottom of the waterfall?

Seek information about the parks at one of the National Park Service visitor centers. In winter you could join a park ranger and learn how to walk on snowshoes. During the summer, the ranger may take you on a walk along a meadow trail.

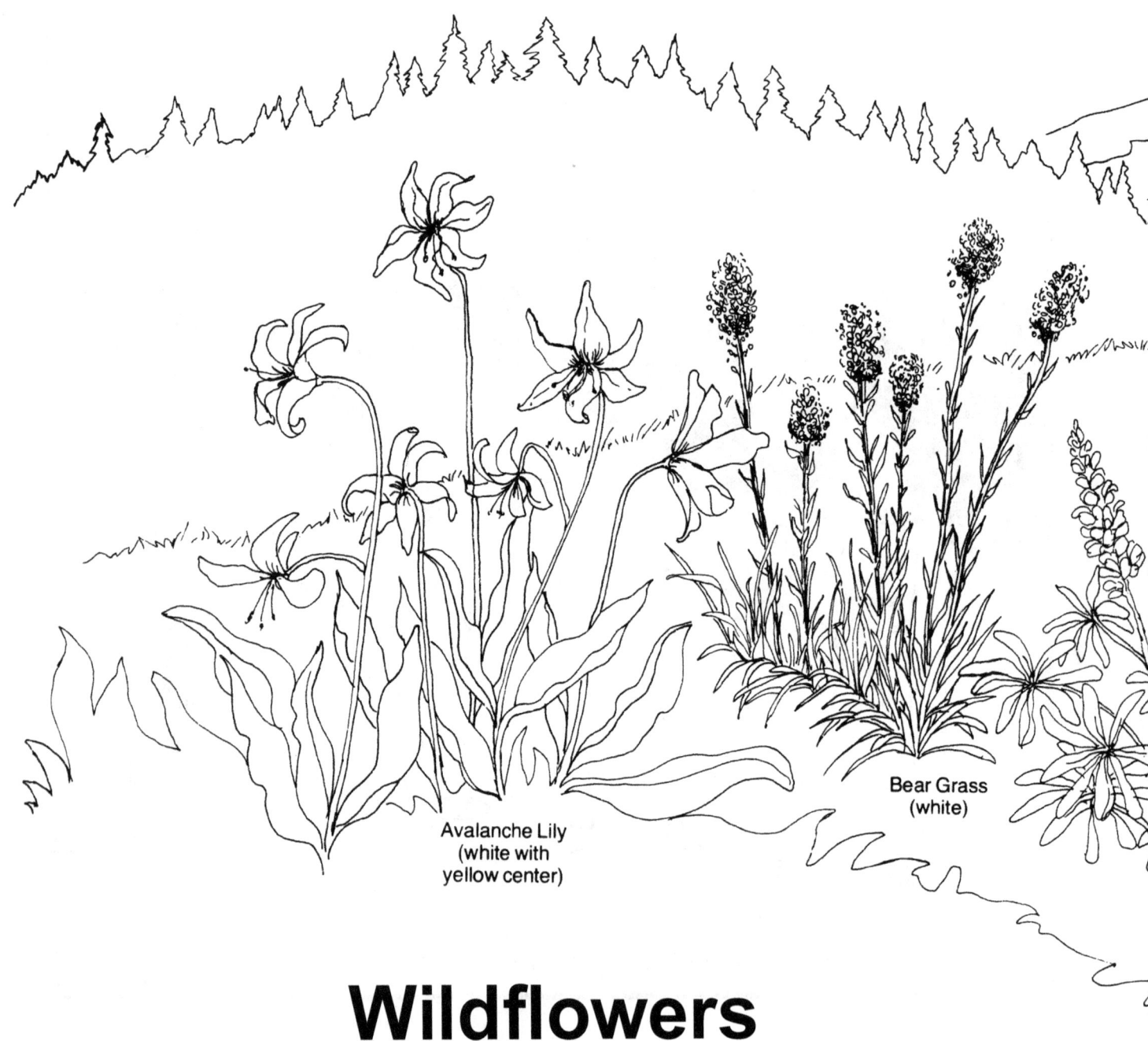

Avalanche Lily
(white with yellow center)

Bear Grass
(white)

Wildflowers

If you walk the high meadow trails in late summer, you will see many wildflowers. Mount Rainier has some of the most beautiful flowers in the world. Some even bloom before the snow melts. Color the flowers.

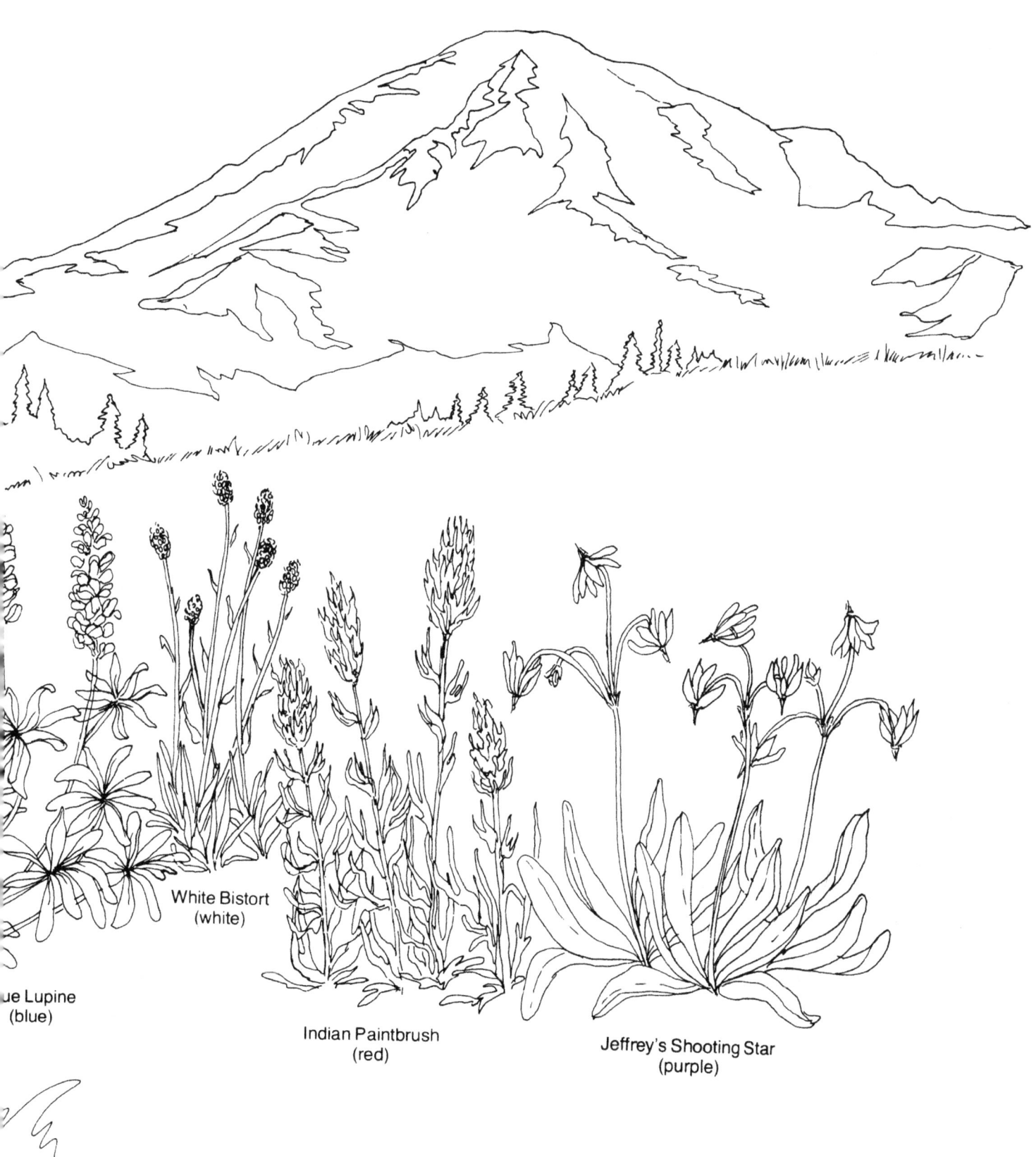

These plants are very delicate or easily hurt. If people or animals walk all over the flowers they may not grow back again for many years. Some are 10 to 15 years old before they bloom. Be sure to stay on the trail.

15

At Paradise Inn, you can have fun watching birds and other animals. Can you tell the difference between the chipmunk and the golden-mantled ground squirrel?

Please do not feed the animals! Even though they may eat the food, it is not the kind they need. If they can get food from people, they will not look for food themselves and may go hungry or starve when people are not there. They may bite too, if they learn not to be afraid of people.

Winter Eater

What do you suppose gathers the little haystacks you see lying on the rocks? These are collected by pikas, which will store the hay under rocks to eat during the winter.

Pika

Winter Sleeper

The marmot gets fat by eating lots of good things during the summer. Then it goes into a deep sleep all winter and lives on its fat. This is called hibernating. You may see the marmot eating wildflowers, which it loves, or hear its whistle nearby.

Marmot

If this were you at Mount Rainier, what would you see? Can you draw the mountain and some of the animals and plants on this page?

Animal Tails

Can you guess which animal owns which tail?

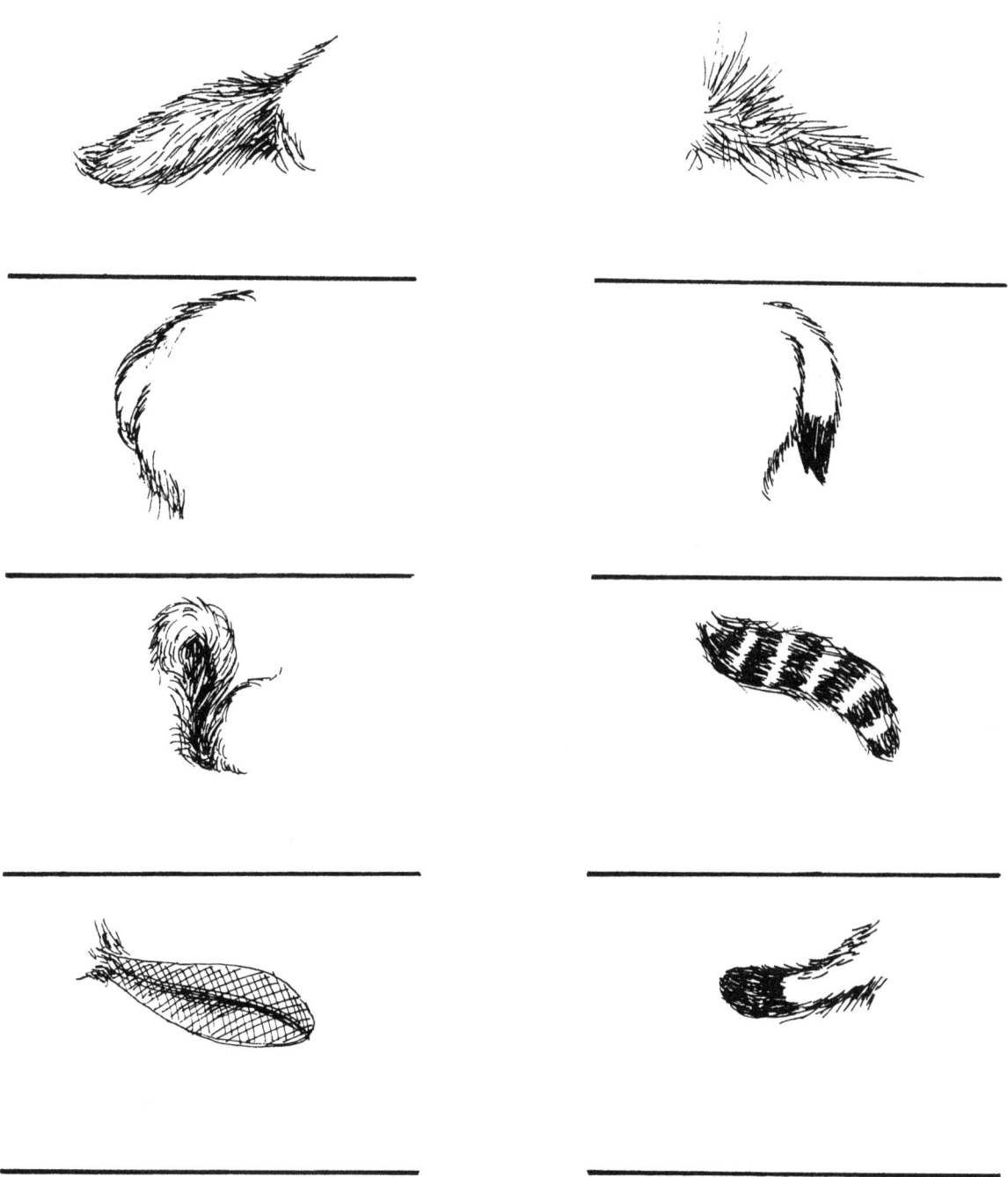

Use the following animals:

Black-tailed deer   Squirrel   Porcupine   Raccoon
Bear   Beaver   Bobcat   Red fox

Closer to the top, sparkling lakes surrounded by meadows or groves of alpine trees make exploring Mount Rainier very exciting. How many of these animals and plants can you find on your trip to the park?

Summer Coats–Winter Coats

Animals often have colors which help them hide from other animals. This is called camouflage. Some even change color. The animals on this page are brownish like the bare ground in the summer and white like snow in the winter.

You

Ptarmigan

Snowshoe Hare

Ermine
or
Short-tailed Weasel

Footprint Detective

If you look closely at the snow or mud, you may see footprints. You can often tell what animal was there and what it was doing. Ask yourself questions like: Is it big or little? Does it have toes? Does it hop? Does it have claws? Was it moving fast?

Can you match these footprints with their owners?

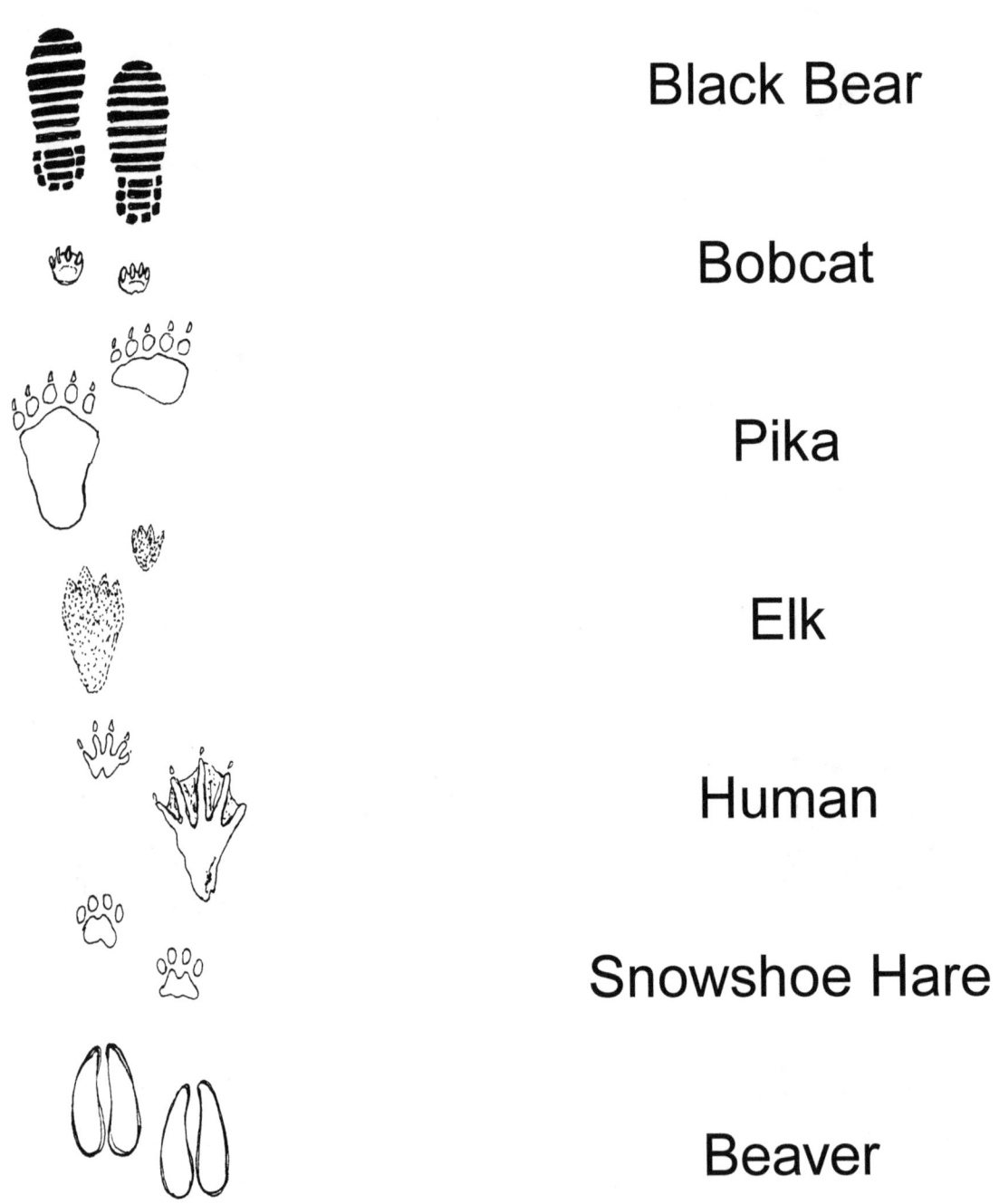

Black Bear

Bobcat

Pika

Elk

Human

Snowshoe Hare

Beaver

Climbers

Mountain goats are natural climbers, living on steep, rugged cliffs and mountain meadows. Their small feet, with wide openings between their toes, give them sure footing on narrow rock shelves and the steepest slopes. Even baby goats, called kids, can climb when only a few hours old.

People like to climb, too. Climbers may leave from Paradise one day and spend the night at Camp Muir before climbing to the top of the mountain the next day. Most people go with a group and guides because it's safer. Why are these climbers tied together with a rope?

The first woman who climbed Mount Rainier wore a long dress and carried a hiking stick.

This climber has finally made it to the top. The good feeling of finishing the climb is not the only reward. On a clear day, people can see that Mount Rainier is surrounded by the beautiful Cascade mountains. It's like being on top of the world and being able to see everything. Climbers see there is much more world to discover.

Glaciers

Snow Falling

Compacting to Ice

Glacier Moves

River from Glacier

Mount Rainier has many glaciers. A glacier is made of lots of snow, which, in time, turns to ice. The ice becomes so thick and heavy that it slips down the mountain, but so slowly we can't see it move. The movement often makes deep cracks called crevasses. The ice scrapes the ground underneath. This is why melting ice from a glacier makes a river that looks muddy.

Chilly Homes

Is there life on glaciers?

Ice worms, looking like little fat hairs, make their homes in holes on the ice. Less than an inch long, they are colored black or bronze-black. The worms eat watermelon algae. The tiny red algae makes the snow look red.

26

Grinding Glaciers

Active glaciers grind rock into powder as the ice slowly moves down the mountain. This powdered rock is called "glacial flour." Glacial flour in the water makes a stream appear dirty. Some people say the water looks like chocolate milk. Streams that start from snow or springs have clear water.

Look at the streams on the picture below. Are they dirty or clear? Trace each stream's flow and write the word "dirty" or "clear" in the circle. The first two are done for you.

Answers: A, D, E, G, J, K, and L are dirty; the rest are clear.

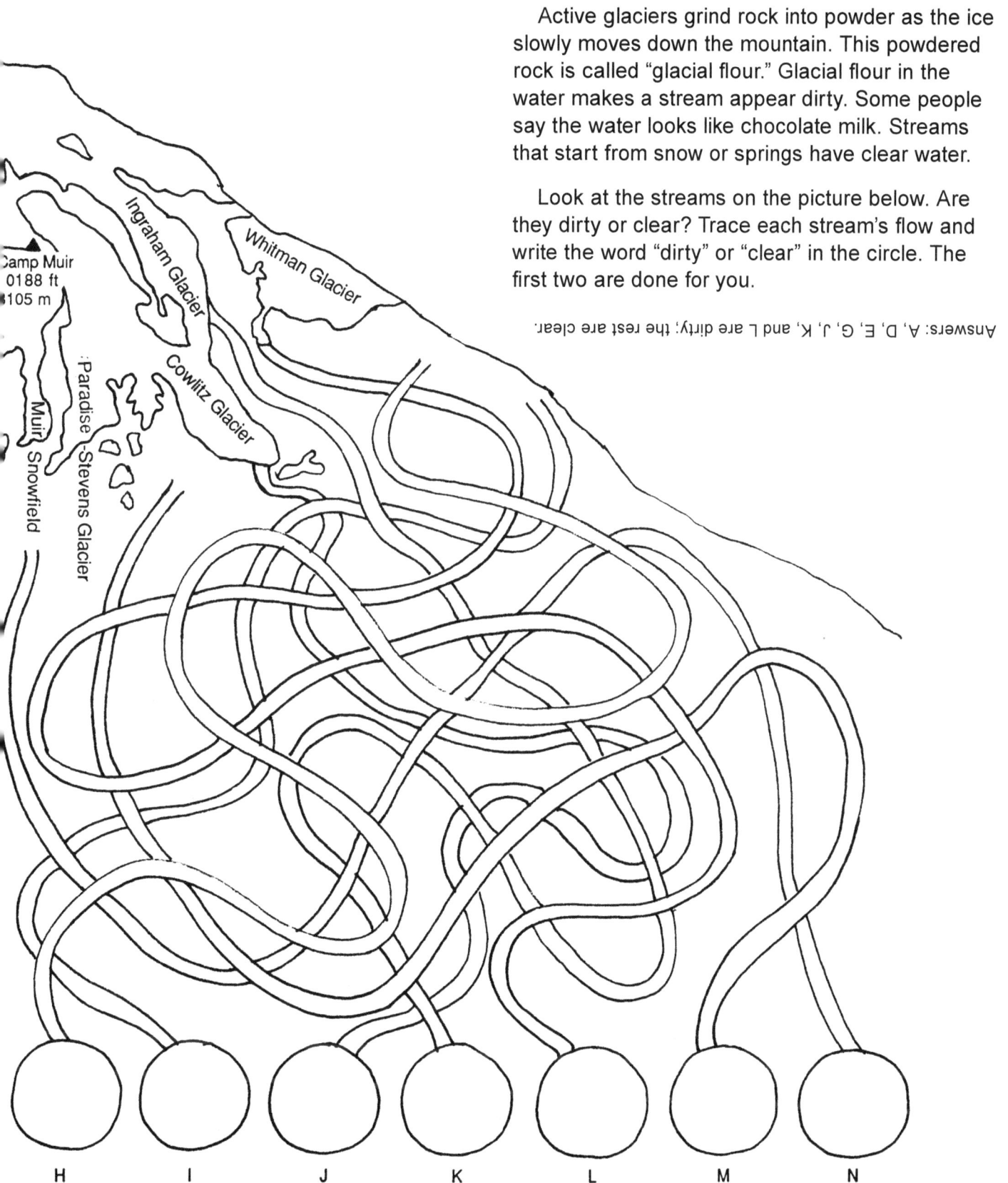

The Glacier's Gift

How does the Nisqually Glacier help the people and wildlife who live miles from the mountain? The answer is that it gives birth to a river. Melting ice from the glacier forms the Nisqually River. The river brings life-giving water to areas below the mountain. It flows from the mountain to the waters of Puget Sound and on out to sea.

Trace the 78 mile route of the Nisqually River up to the headwaters at the glacier. Unscramble the words you meet along the way to find out how the river benefits both people and wildlife.

Answers upside down bottom of page

2. hisf ychtaehr
_____
Protected Waters along the river are good places for raising fish. Salmon are raised for sport and commercial fishing.

3. inloggg
_____
Forests near the river keep the water cool, clean, and healthy. With careful planning, some trees can be harvested.

4. oswnt
_____
People have always built their homes close to rivers. They provide drinking water, transportation, and food.

Waters of Puget Sound

Nisqually River

1. idlwiefl eurfeg
_____
Wildlife is plentiful in the wetlands and forests at the mouth of the river. Many kinds of sea life are found in the waters of the Nisqually National Wildlife Refuge.

5. ganfirm
_____
Flood waters lay down good soil for growing crops.

28

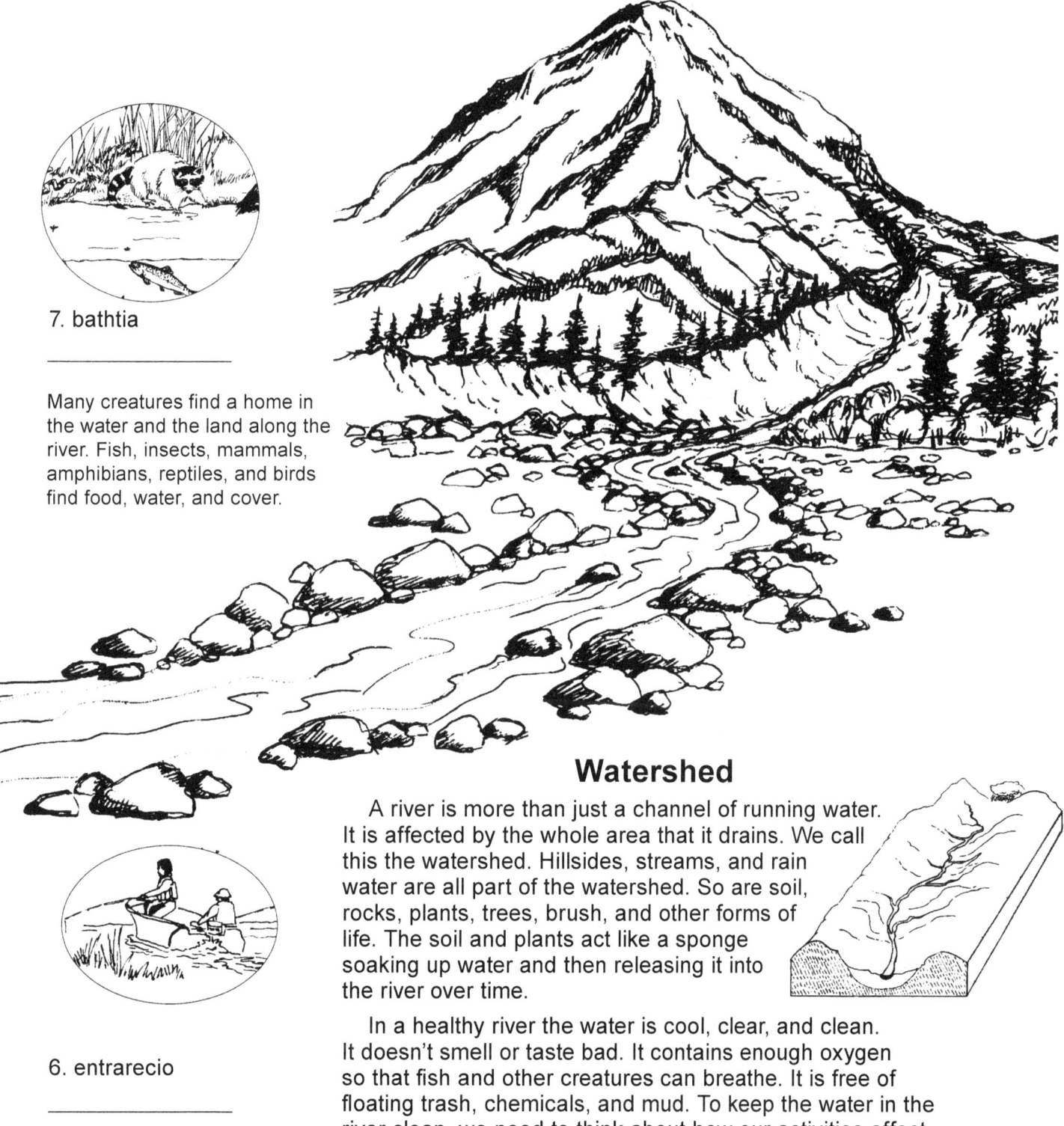

7. bathtia

_____

Many creatures find a home in the water and the land along the river. Fish, insects, mammals, amphibians, reptiles, and birds find food, water, and cover.

6. entrarecio

_____

People swim, boat, and fish in the waters. They watch birds and take pictures.

Watershed

A river is more than just a channel of running water. It is affected by the whole area that it drains. We call this the watershed. Hillsides, streams, and rain water are all part of the watershed. So are soil, rocks, plants, trees, brush, and other forms of life. The soil and plants act like a sponge soaking up water and then releasing it into the river over time.

In a healthy river the water is cool, clear, and clean. It doesn't smell or taste bad. It contains enough oxygen so that fish and other creatures can breathe. It is free of floating trash, chemicals, and mud. To keep the water in the river clean, we need to think about how our activities affect the quality of the water in the river. If we don't take good care of the entire watershed, we can spoil the river for wildlife and for ourselves.

Answers: 1. wildlife refuge 2. fish hatchery 3. logging 4. towns 5. farming 6. recreation 7. habitat

The Cascade Mountains

Mount Rainier is part of a circle of volcanoes, called the Ring of Fire, on the edges of land surrounding the Pacific Ocean. It is found in the Cascade Mountain range which runs from British Columbia, Canada to California.

Some volcanoes are awake and erupt fairly regularly. They are called active. Others are sleeping or dormant, but could erupt again sometime. Mount Rainier is a dormant volcano.

Can you name the volcanoes on the map below?

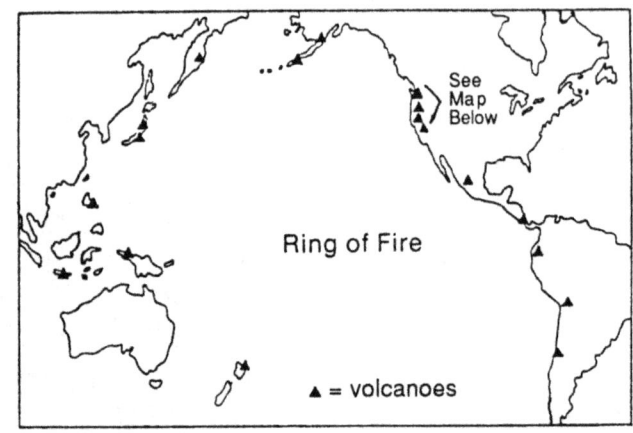

See Map Below
Ring of Fire
▲ = volcanoes

Answers at bottom of page.

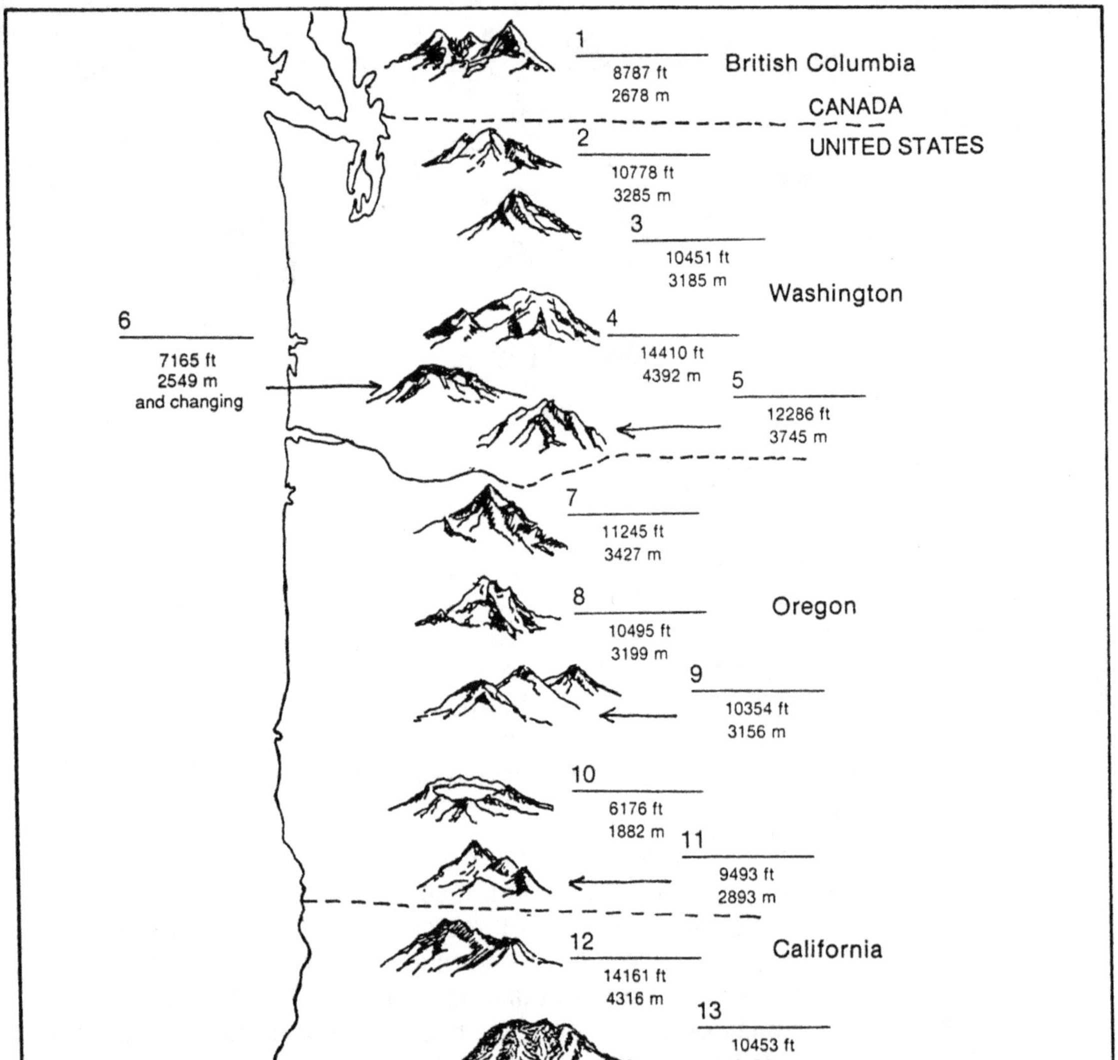

1
8787 ft
2678 m
British Columbia
CANADA
UNITED STATES
2
10778 ft
3285 m
3
10451 ft
3185 m
Washington
4
14410 ft
4392 m
6
7165 ft
2549 m
and changing
5
12286 ft
3745 m
7
11245 ft
3427 m
Oregon
8
10495 ft
3199 m
9
10354 ft
3156 m
10
6176 ft
1882 m
11
9493 ft
2893 m
California
12
14161 ft
4316 m
13
10453 ft
3186 m

1. Mt. Garibaldi; 2. Mt. Baker; 3. Glacier Peak; 4. Mount Rainier; 5. Mt. Adams; 6. Mount St. Helens; 7. Mt. Hood; 8. Mt. Jefferson; 9. Three Sisters; 10. Crater Lake; 11. Mt. McLoughlin; 12. Mt. Shasta; 13. Lassen Peak

Inside Mount Rainier

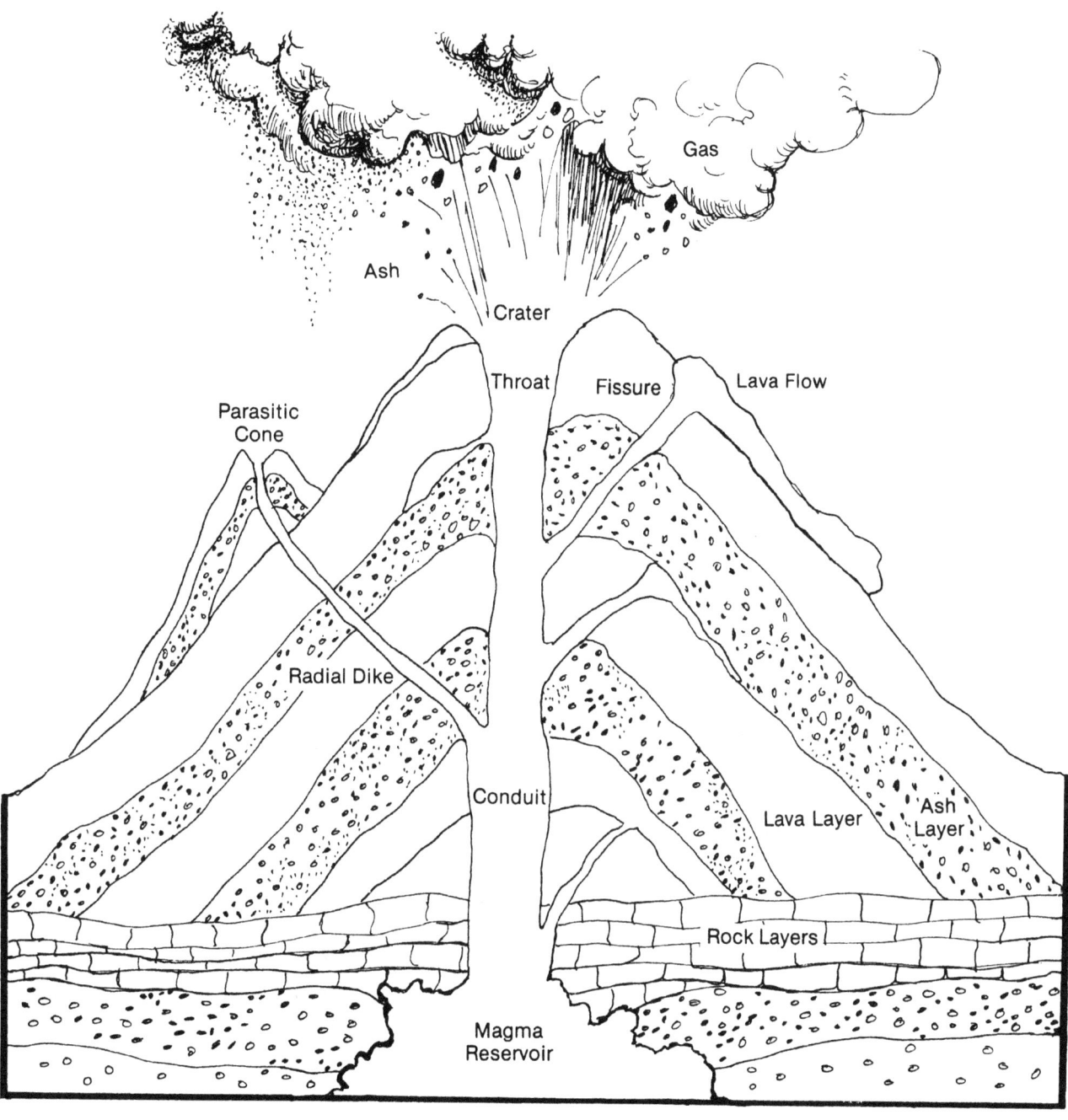

Mount Rainier formed over a very long period of time in a series of volcanic eruptions. Sometimes magma, molten or melted rock, flowed out of the volcano. When the magma flowed out of the mountain, it was called lava. Other times, the volcano erupted more violently. Gases and tiny particles of ash were blown out. Layer after layer of lava and ash make up Mount Rainier. This type of volcano is called a composite or stratovolcano.

The last eruption of Mount Rainier was about 2000 years ago. The most recent eruption probably happened within the past 150 to 200 years.

Mount Rainier Bingo

See how many bingos you and your friends can get by marking off the things you see in Mount Rainier National Park.

Inside Mount Rainier

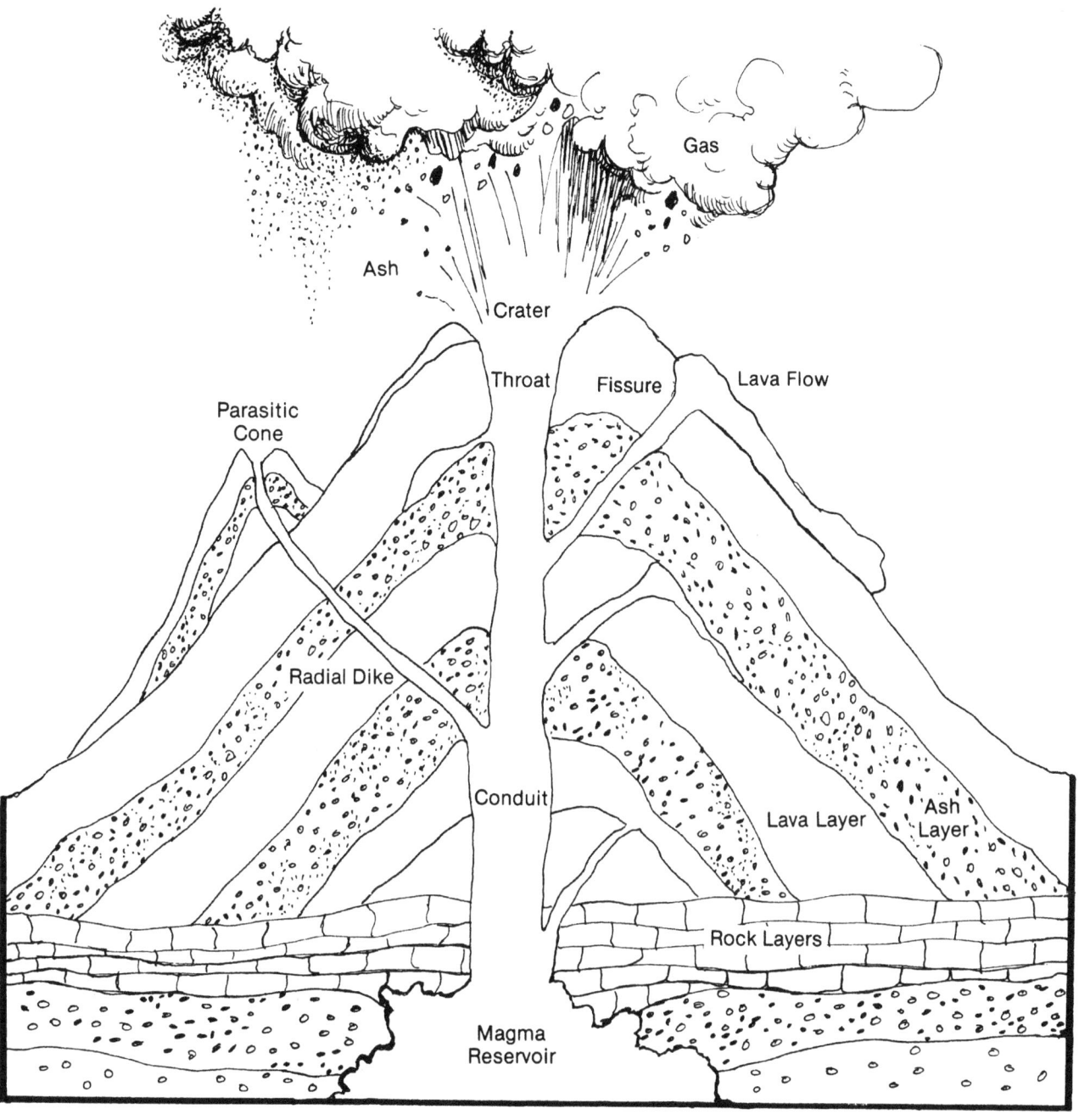

Mount Rainier formed over a very long period of time in a series of volcanic eruptions. Sometimes magma, molten or melted rock, flowed out of the volcano. When the magma flowed out of the mountain, it was called lava. Other times, the volcano erupted more violently. Gases and tiny particles of ash were blown out. Layer after layer of lava and ash make up Mount Rainier. This type of volcano is called a composite or stratovolcano.

The last eruption of Mount Rainier was about 2000 years ago. The most recent eruption probably happened within the past 150 to 200 years.

Mount Rainier Bingo

See how many bingos you and your friends can get by marking off the things you see in Mount Rainier National Park.

CPSIA information can be obtained
at www.ICGtesting.com
Printed in the USA
LVHW060746140222
711073LV00007B/266